"RELIGIOUS GLADIATORS"

- Beware of Contemporary Judaizers -

Julio A. Rodriguez

"Beloved, when I gave all diligence to write unto you of the common salvation, it was needful for me to write unto you, and exhort *you* that ye should earnestly contend for the faith which was once delivered unto the saints"

(Jude 3)

"RELIGIOUS GLADIATORS"

- Beware of Contemporary Judaizers –

© **Copyright 2010**   Julio A. Rodriguez

All Rights Reserved.

ISBN-10   0977934993

ISBN-13   978-0-9779349-9-7

The scriptural quotations are taken from King James Version (KJV)

Translated by: Frank Mercado Siuro

First Edition published in Spanish on November 2010; and in English, on March 2011

Editorial Nueva Vida

53-21 37 Ave., Woodside, NY   11377

Tel: 718-205-5111

To be classified as: Sects, Discipleship and Biblical Doctrine

Printed in United States of America.

Contents:

Prologue

I am grateful to the Lord for allowing me to read this book. I believe many will be blessed in they desire to please God and comprehend his plan for mankind. They will not be disappointed, and be equipped to resist and stand firm against those that distort the truth of the gospel.

The publication is timely as we confront the "plague" of perverted teaching that has contaminated the church in this post-modern age. Many believers have stumbled and even fallen into this trap.

My prayer is that those who yearn to be familiar with Jewish tradition and still remain faithful to the church of Christ find this book of great use and edification. We hope and pray that those already carried away and deceived will allow themselves to enter the light of the glorious truth of who we are in Christ, and return to the Good Shepherd who loves them.

Many are being seduced by a power from the enemy of our souls and the world stands ready to accuse the church, as they witness the strife and division in contemporary Christianity. Some say, "They don't agree on anything and are always divided." We should intercede in prayer and ask the Lord for wisdom to discern, and recognize the signs of these end times.

I praise God for the ministry of Pastor Julio Rodriguez and his obedience to the voice and calling of God. He has willingly placed himself available to God and as an instrument of honor stands as a watchman ready to teach, pray, and contend for the faith. He has not hesitated to challenge false teaching that may infiltrate and confuse the faithful.

More than anything, I thank Jesus Christ. My appreciation for what he did for me on the cross has increased, and I value more than anything that it was his suffering that made me free from the condemnation of the law. I praise Him for His love and mercy towards me.

By his grace I can live in peace with God and be confident in his presence. Jesus Christ is the way to draw near to our heavenly Father.

Thank you, Jesus!

Pr. Leonor Rodriguez

Introduction

I have great personal admiration for the descendants of Israel. They have demonstrated a clear and undeniable identity throughout the centuries, have unifying customs, emphasized childhood education, demonstrated abundant scientific capacity, have loved God intensely, etc.

The Lord Jesus spoke of them:

> "...for salvation is of the Jews." (John 4:22)[i]

The Apostle Paul said of Israel:

> "...Who are Israelites; to whom [pertaineth] the adoption, and the glory, and the covenants, and the giving of the law, and the service [of God], and the promises. Whose [are] the fathers, and of whom as concerning the flesh Christ [came], who is over all, God blessed for ever. Amen" (Romans 9:4-5)

Apostle Peter exhorted the Jews:

> "For the promise is unto you, and to your children, and to all that are afar off, [even] as many as the Lord our God shall call." (Acts 2:39)

The Jewish people came forth as a manifestation of the power of God through elderly Abram and his beloved wife Sarah, who was sterile and past the time of child bearing. The indestructible faith of Abraham was honored and a testimony was given to all mankind that would inhabit the earth., that God is the giver of all life, the only true and exalted God; Creator of all things. He is Omnipotent and for whom nothing is impossible...

The Hebrew people deserve the recognition of all nations as a real gift from God for humanity. Their documented history has revealed the character, will, and purpose of God for all mankind.

Their significant contributions to science have impacted us in developing and forming the intellectual impetus in modern societies today, thru God's grace.

The ratio of Nobel laureates in proportion to Jewish population in the world speaks for itself. They have been awarded over 20% of all Nobel prizes, although they are approximately one- fifth of one percent of the total world population *(14 million out of a world population total of approx. 6.2 billion).*

They have been so privileged on the part of God that from 1901 to 2008, more than 170 Jewish people received the Nobel Prize.

The following is a comparative analysis:

- Chemistry - 30 awards; equivalent to 20 % of the worldwide total
- Economics - 26 awards; equivalent to 42 % of the worldwide total
- Literature - 13 awards; equivalent to 12 % of worldwide total
- Peace Prize - 9 awards; equivalent to 9 % of world wide total
- Physics- 47 awards; equivalent to 26 % of world wide total
- Philosophy &Medicine - 47 awards; equivalent to 26 % Of total world wide

I pray on their behalf and offer supplications for the peace of Jerusalem with an honest and sincere affection. My desire before God is that all should come to the knowledge of the truth concerning Jesus Christ, the Messiah of Israel.

Those truly Jewish *(legitimate heirs; **born from the womb** of a Jewish mother)* do not presently proselytize amongst other nations or religions, not seeking converts to Judaism.

Simply stated, they are descendants of the patriarch Abraham and despite the multiple attacks against them and persecutions throughout history, they have persevered giving abundant testimony to the veracity of

8

the written Word revealed in the Holy and Sacred Scriptures.

Many legitimate Jews are now believing and accepting Jesus (Yeshua) as Messiah. They are known as; **Messianic Jews**

The following is extremely important as I will present what is taking place, as many who claim alleged empathy for the Jewish faith are provoking *(even pretending to be Jews without validity, not being born of a Jewish mother)* in different nations of the world; in detriment of the true gospel message of faith in Christ.

It is these persons that I will name "THE CONTEMPORARY JUDAIZERS"; or as defined by the Apostle Paul:

> "...false brethren unawares brought in, who came in privily to spy out our liberty which we have in Christ Jesus, which they might bring us into bondage."
>
> (Galatians 2:4)

They profess to be knowledgeable in Jewish customs and beliefs and enter Christian congregations *(who naturally respect and esteem Jewish people)* under the pretext of teaching "real" Jewish culture.

They then confuse and attempt to convince those that listen to assimilate Jewishness and renounce their Christian faith. They claim that *"if one wishes to partake of the promises given in the Bible and truly be a part of God's people*, it is required to live as a Jew in all ways."

This has sown much confusion amongst believers and in many instances some have turned from the true path and suffered grave consequences.

They invalidate grace and forfeit blessings, as the **Apostle Paul** (Saul of Tarsus; Apostle of the gentiles) wrote:

> "Christ is become of no effect unto you, whosoever of you are justified by the law; **ye are fallen from grace.**" (Gal 5:4)[ii]

> **"Ye observe days, and months, and times, and years**. I am afraid of you, lest I have bestowed upon you labor in vain." (Gal 4: 10-11)

> "So then they which be of faith are blessed with faithful Abraham. For as many as are of the works of the law **are under the curse**: for it is written, Cursed [is] every one that continues not in all things which are written in the book of the law to do them."
>
> (Gal 3: 9-10)

This word is fortified in the call of **Apostle Jude** when he writes:

> "Beloved, when I gave all diligence to write unto you of the common salvation, it was needful for me to write unto you, and exhort [you] that **ye should earnestly contend for the faith** which was once delivered unto the saints." (Jude 3)

In addition we have the admonition of **Apostle Peter**:

> "But there were false prophets also among the people, even as there shall be false teachers among you, <u>who privily shall bring in damnable heresies</u>, even denying the Lord that bought them, and bring upon themselves swift destruction." (2 Peter 2:1)

We read this warning from **Apostle Paul**:

> "Take heed therefore unto yourselves, and to all the flock, over the which the Holy Ghost hath made you overseers, to feed the church of God, which he hath purchased with his own blood.

> For I know this, that after my departing **shall grievous wolves enter in among you,** not sparing the flock. *Also of your own selves shall men arise, speaking perverse things, to draw away disciples after them"* (Acts 20: 28-30)

I echo the words of Apostle Paul in his Epistle to the Ephesians:

> "That the God of our Lord Jesus Christ, the Father of glory, may give unto you the spirit of wisdom and revelation in the knowledge of him: The eyes of your understanding being enlightened; **that ye may know what is the hope of his calling**, and what the riches of the glory of his inheritance in the saints, And what is the exceeding greatness of his power to usward who believe, according to the working of his mighty power..." (Ephesians 1: 17-19)

The Judaizers have sown confusion with respect to who are the "people of God."

They debate this while being exclusive. The Bible speaks to us of one body in Christ. There is neither Jew nor Greek, but all those that believe in Jesus Christ and the efficacy of the Cross are redeemed.

THE COVENANT ESTABLISHED

In this chapter we will cover primarily the significance of the covenant God has established with His people Israel and further focus on how we, as the Ekklesia (Church), have benefited from the sacrifice and victory of Christ on the cross. This covenant has been sealed by the precious blood that flowed at Calvary.

Let us examine the Holy Scriptures and what is written concerning us, the Body of Christ, and in this manner form a solid foundation and be able to….

> "But sanctify the Lord God in your hearts: and be ready always to give an answer to every man that asketh you a reason of the hope that is in you with meekness and fear" (1 Peter 3:15)

It is of utmost importance we remain constant and not allow ourselves to be confounded by those that may enter into our midst with strange doctrines, messengers of another gospel not revealed by the Lord Jesus, nor preached by the Jewish Apostle Paul. He speaks of them:

> "Which is not another; but there be some that trouble you, and would pervert the gospel of Christ. But though we, or an angel from heaven, preach any

13

other gospel unto you than that which we have preached unto you, let him be accursed.

As we said before, so say I now again, If any man preach any other gospel unto you than that ye have received, let him be accursed." (Galatians 1: 7-9)

The history of the Hebrew people, called and chosen by God as His special people on this earth begins in the book of Genesis when God tells Abraham:

"And when Abram was ninety years old and nine, the LORD appeared to Abram, and said unto him, I am the Almighty God; walk before me, and be thou perfect. And I will make my covenant between me and thee, and will multiply thee exceedingly."

"And I will establish my covenant between me and thee and thy seed after thee in their generations for an everlasting covenant, to be a God unto thee, and to thy seed after thee.

And I will give unto thee and to thy seed after thee, the land wherein thou art a stranger, all the land of Canaan, for an everlasting possession; and I will be their God. And God said unto Abraham, Thou shalt keep my covenant therefore, thou, and thy seed after thee in their generations." (Genesis 17:1-2, 7-9)

14

We read that when God called Abraham and told him to walk upright before Him and be perfect, the purpose was to establish a covenant with Him that would extend to all his descendants. The covenant promised that God would watch over them, bless and provide for them, etc. Of all the nations on the earth, they would be His people and a treasure to Him always.

THE FIRST SIGN OF THE COVENANT

The following verses we read declare the conditions of the covenant:

> "This is my covenant, which ye shall keep, between me and you and thy seed after thee; every man child among you **shall be circumcised**." (Genesis 17:10)

The key word in the covenant is "circumcision."

God tells him:

> "And ye shall circumcise the flesh of your foreskin; and it shall be **a token of the covenant** betwixt me and you." (Verse 11)

15

When a Jewish man-child is born and is circumcised as God had instructed, he is considered part of the chosen people as promised to Abraham. He would be their God.

The covenant established with them is an "everlasting" covenant. In this context *everlasting* means:

+ *"It continues forever and will never end."*

The next scripture passages detail who, when, and how the child should be circumcised:

> "And he that is **eight days** old shall be circumcised among you, every man child in your generations, he that is born in the house, or bought with money of any stranger, which is not of thy seed. He that is born in thy house, and he that is bought with thy money, must needs be circumcised: and my covenant shall be in your flesh for an everlasting covenant."
>
> (Genesis 17:12-13)

The act of circumcision was so significant that the male infant that is not circumcised as God has ordained, "Shall be cut off," (vs.14) meaning that he will not be counted as part of the chosen people. The importance of conserving the identity of the people of Israel is part of the act and ritual of circumcision, being performed on the eighth day on faithful Abraham's posterity.

16

However, the fact that Israel is God's chosen people does not exclude them from times of suffering. God himself foretold Abraham:

> "And he said unto Abram, Know of a surety that thy seed shall be a stranger in a land that is not theirs, and shall serve them; and they shall afflict them four hundred years; And also that nation, whom they shall serve, will I judge: and afterward shall they come out with great substance." (Genesis 15: 13-14)

This word was fulfilled and we can read the narrative in the Book of Exodus:

> "...And Joseph died, and all his brethren, and all that generation. [And the children of Israel were fruitful, and increased abundantly, and multiplied, and waxed exceeding mighty; and the land was filled with them.
>
> ...Now there arose up a new king over Egypt, which knew not Joseph....
>
> ... And the Egyptians made the children of Israel to serve with rigour: And they made their lives bitter with hard bondage, in morter, and in brick, and in all manner of service in the field: all their service, wherein they made them serve, was with rigour"
>
> (Exodus 1: 6-14)

Further on we read:

> "And it came to pass in process of time, that the king
> of Egypt died: and the children of Israel sighed by
> reason of the bondage, and they cried, and their cry
> came up unto God by reason of the bondage.
>
> And God heard their groaning, and God <u>remembered</u>
> <u>his covenant with Abraham</u>, with Isaac, and with
> Jacob. And God looked upon the children of Israel, and
> God had respect unto them." (Exodus 2:23-25)

Yahweh (Lord- I AM) then appears to Moses and sends
him on the mission to liberate His people from bondage to
the Egyptians:

> "Moreover he said, I am the God of thy father, the God
> of Abraham, the God of Isaac, and the God of Jacob ...
> Now therefore, behold, the cry of the children of Israel
> is come unto me: and I have also seen the oppression
> wherewith the Egyptians oppress them...
>
> Come now therefore, and I will send thee unto
> Pharaoh, that thou mayest bring forth my people the
> children of Israel out of Egypt." (Exodus 3:6-10)

THE SECOND SIGN OF THE COVENANT

The Bible narrative tells us of **second sign**; apart from circumcision that was to identify His people that had escaped from Egypt. This would be **the blood** shed during Passover.

Exodus 12: 1-28 relates to us how after the Hebrew people are led from Egypt by Moses the Passover celebration is instituted. Moses receives the details from God of how the animal should be chosen, the time of the calendar year chosen, and how to fulfill all God's instructions to perfection.

He also tells Moses:

> "And ye shall observe this thing for an ordinance to thee and to thy sons forever. And it shall come to pass, when ye be come to the land which the LORD will give you, according as he hath promised, that ye shall keep this service." (Exodus 12:24-25)

A commandment is given and **this new ritual** is celebrated **annually** by the Hebrew nation. It was established as an eternal ordinance between God and his people, in remembrance of their deliverance.

We read of Moses when he gathered the people on Mount Sinai:

> "Moses wrote all the words of the LORD, and rose up early in the morning, and builded an altar under the hill, and twelve pillars, according to the twelve tribes of Israel. And he sent young men of the children of Israel, which offered burnt offerings, and sacrificed peace offerings of oxen unto the LORD.
>
> And Moses took half of the blood, and put it in basons; **and half of the blood he sprinkled on the altar**. And he took the book of the covenant, and read in the audience of the people: and they said, All that the LORD hath said will we do, and be obedient.
>
> And Moses took the blood, and sprinkled it on the people, and said, **Behold the blood** of the covenant, which the LORD hath made with you concerning all these words" (Exodus 24: 4-8)

On that day a covenant of blood was established between God and His people with Moses as an intermediary. This was an eternal covenant. The High Priest was to sacrifice an animal once a year on the "Day of Atonement."

The priest was an intermediary between God and His people and would pour out the blood of the slain animal that was without spot or blemish as a sin offering for all the transgressions of the people in the prior year

- The blood shed and presented to God is the sign of the covenant, or pact, between God and His people.

The pact between God and Israel **was mutual** and both sides would have to honor this pact. It is imperative to understand that any agreement has to be adhered to by **both parties** to remain valid. One side is insufficient to continue the pact and both must stay true

God is faithful and cannot violate His word. He will always do what He promises and expects the same of us. We must keep our word and our promises.

What happened to Israel? Why did the children of Israel fall short, doubt, and violate the pact with their God?

In disobedience they offended God and made a mockery of the Omnipotent God with whom they had promised loyalty.

"Go thou near, and hear all that the LORD our God shall say: and speak thou unto us all that the LORD our God shall speak unto thee; and **we will hear it, and do it**." (Deuteronomy 5:27)

Jeremiah later wrote:

"...Thus saith the LORD of hosts, the God of Israel; Put your burnt offerings unto your sacrifices, and eat flesh. For I spake not unto your fathers, nor commanded them in the day that I brought them out of the land of Egypt, concerning burnt offerings or sacrifices: But this thing commanded I them, saying, Obey my voice, and I will be your God, and ye shall be my people: and walk ye in all the ways that I have commanded you, that it may be well unto you.

But they hearkened not, nor inclined their ear, but walked in the counsels and in the imagination of their evil heart, and went backward, and not forward. Since the day that your fathers came forth out of the land of Egypt unto this day I have even sent unto you all my servants the prophets, daily rising up early and sending them:

Yet they hearkened not unto me, nor inclined their ear, but hardened their neck: they did worse than their fathers." (Jeremiah: 7:21-26)

It is disconcerting to realize that Almighty God, who always seeks our well being, is obligated to speak against His own people with such severity. The righteous judgment of God must expose our disobedience and rebellion.

In this respect the Bible says:

> "And the LORD God of their fathers sent to them by his messengers, rising up betimes, and sending; because he had compassion on his people, and on his dwelling place: But they mocked the messengers of God, and despised his words, and misused his prophets, **until the wrath of the LORD arose against his people, till there was no remedy**.
>
> Therefore he brought upon them the king of the Chaldees, who slew their young men with the sword in the house of their sanctuary, and had no compassion upon young man or maiden, old man, or him that stooped for age: he gave them all into his hand. And all the vessels of the house of God, great and small, and the treasures of the house of the LORD, and the treasures of the king, and of his princes; all these he brought to Babylon.
>
> And they burnt the house of God, and brake down the wall of Jerusalem, and burnt all the palaces thereof with fire,

and destroyed all the goodly vessels thereof. And them that had escaped from the sword carried he away to Babylon; where they were servants to him and his sons until the reign of the kingdom of Persia:" (2 Chronicles 36:15-20)

Those that know not God; in reflection may judge this penalty as harsh and cruel, thinking justice was not really served. Nevertheless, we who know Him have experienced is grace and the beauty of his holiness, acknowledging that he is Wonderful and his ways are beyond reproach. (see Job). The Prophet Ezra writes of this later in the Holy Scriptures:

"Yet many years didst thou forbear them, and testifiedst against them by thy spirit in thy prophets: yet would they not give ear: therefore gavest thou them into the hand of the people of the lands. Nevertheless for thy great mercies' sake thou didst not utterly consume them, nor forsake them; for thou art a gracious and merciful God.

Now therefore, our God, the great, the mighty, and the terrible God, **who keepest covenant and mercy**, let not all the trouble seem little before thee, that hath come upon us, on our kings, on our princes, and on our priests, and on our prophets, and on our fathers, and on all thy people, since the time of the kings of Assyria unto this day. **Howbeit thou art just** in all that is brought upon us; for **thou hast done right**, but we have done wickedly:

Neither have our kings, our princes, our priests, nor our fathers, kept thy law, nor hearkened unto thy commandments and thy testimonies, wherewith thou didst testify against them. For they have not served thee in their kingdom, and in thy great goodness that thou gavest them, and in the large and fat land which thou gavest before them, neither turned they from their wicked works." (Nehemiah 9: 30-35)

We read that the mercies of God are abundant and He remembers our affliction. He desires to restore His people, though they suffer judgment for a season. After judging those of Israel who had broken the covenant sealed by blood, He offered the remnant in Israel that remained and were spared a "new covenant."

The power of this new covenant, or pact, will enable them to fulfill it, and never again suffer destruction as their fathers had.

Jeremiah writes prophetically in the Spirit:

"Behold, the days come, saith the LORD, that I will make a new covenant with the house of Israel, and with the house of Judah: Not according to the

25

covenant that I made with their fathers in the day that I took them by the hand to bring them out of the land of Egypt; **which my covenant they brake**, although I was an husband unto them, saith the LORD:

But this shall be the covenant that I will make with the house of Israel; After those days, saith the LORD, <u>I will put my law in their inward parts, and write it in their hearts</u>; and will be their God, and they shall be my people.

And they shall teach no more every man his neighbour, and every man his brother, saying, Know the LORD: for they shall all know me, from the least of them unto the greatest of them, saith the LORD; for I will forgive their iniquity, and I will remember their sin no more." (Jeremiah 31: 31-34)

God declares that the covenant made with Moses as the mediator was **broken by His people**. They were disobedient and violated the conditions given. It was **now void** before Him. Those that disobeyed perished under the heavy hands of the Assyrians, Babylonians, and others, as recorded in the Holy Scriptures. Judgment came and sudden destruction soon followed. All the people **did not perish** and to **those that remained** He declares, "a new covenant shall I establish with you."

WE NOTE HERE: The covenant of circumcision is not mentioned and to this day Israel continues this practice. The covenant with Abraham was not violated. The pact with Moses as the intermediary was violated as the people followed not the law (Torah) and departed from the commandments and ordinances given. They did not keep them with all their heart and remain in a covenant relationship.

Now God speaks again to the people that He will establish a covenant "sealed by blood" but it will be new and different. It will not be as that one that was made when the people were delivered from Egypt. He says, "This time I will not give you a law written on tablets of stone but I will write my law in your hearts so you understand and keep it."

The Holy Bible shows us that God will take on human form and come to earth to fulfill all the conditions of the law:

> "Therefore the Lord himself shall give you a sign; Behold, a virgin shall conceive, and bear a son, and shall call his name **Immanuel**." (Isaiah 7:14)

+ Emmanuel is interpreted as "**God with us**"

Other characteristics given to the child prophesied that would be born are:

> "...and the government shall be upon his shoulder: and his name shall be called Wonderful, Counselor, The **mighty God**, The **everlasting Father**, The Prince of Peace." (Isaiah 9:6)

We also read in Scripture:

> "...**The spirit of the LORD shall rest upon him,** the spirit of wisdom and understanding, the spirit of counsel and might, the spirit of knowledge and of the fear of the LORD" (Isaiah 11: 2)

The main purpose for the birth of the child born of a virgin would be: Take on himself our afflictions, bear our grieves, be wounded for our transgressions, he was bruised for our iniquities, the chastisement of our peace was upon him... when thou shalt make his soul an offering for sin

> "Surely he hath borne our griefs, and carried our sorrows: yet we did esteem him stricken, smitten of God, and afflicted.
>
> But he was wounded for our transgressions; he was bruised for our iniquities: the chastisement of our peace was upon him; and with his stripes we are

healed. All we like sheep have gone astray; we have turned every one to his own way; and the LORD hath laid on him the iniquity of us all."

"Yet it pleased the LORD to bruise him; he hath put him to grief: when thou shalt make his soul an offering for sin, he shall see his seed, he shall prolong his days, and the pleasure of the LORD shall prosper in his hand." (Isaiah 53: 4-6, 10)

We will examine the fulfillment of the promise...

The Bible says that Jesus Christ the only begotten Son of God came as a mediator between God and men. This is the new covenant.

It is written in the Word of God:

"In the beginning was the **Word**, and the Word was with God, and the Word **was God...** He was in the world, and the world was made by him, and the world knew him not. He came unto his own, and his own received him not..."

"And the Word was made flesh, and dwelt among us, (and we beheld his glory, the glory as of the only begotten of the Father,) full of grace and truth."
(John1:1, 10-11, 14)

"Let this mind be in you, which was also in **Christ Jesus**: Who, being in the form of God, thought it not robbery **to be equal with God**:

But made himself of no reputation, and took upon him the form of a servant, and was made in the likeness of men: And being found in fashion as a man, he humbled himself, and **became obedient unto death**, even the death of the cross." (Philippians 2: 5-8)

The Bible tells us that the **Word of God** was born of a virgin named Mary (Miriam):

"And in the sixth month the angel Gabriel was sent from God unto a city of Galilee, named Nazareth, To a virgin espoused to a man whose name was Joseph, of the house of David; and the virgin's name was Mary.

And the angel came in unto her, and said, Hail, thou that art highly favoured, the Lord is with thee: blessed art thou among women. And when she saw him, she was troubled at his saying, and cast in her mind what manner of salutation this should be.

And the angel said unto her, Fear not, Mary: for thou hast found favour with God. And, behold, thou shalt conceive in thy womb, and bring forth a son, and shalt call his name JESUS. He shall be great, and shall be

30

called the Son of the Highest: and the Lord God shall give unto him the throne of his father David: And he shall reign over the house of Jacob for ever; and of his kingdom there shall be no end.

Then said Mary unto the angel, How shall this be, seeing I know not a man? And the angel answered and said unto her, The Holy Ghost shall come upon thee, and the power of the Highest shall overshadow thee: therefore also that holy thing which shall be born of thee shall be called the Son of God." (Luke 1: 26-35)

Jesus Christ was born during the reign of the Roman emperor Augustus Caesar and lived a blameless life before God (See Luke 2: 1-7) Jesus himself inquired of the Jewish leaders, *"Which one of you accuseth me of sin?"* (John 8: 46); He also said. "...the prince of this world cometh, **and hath nothing in me**." (John 14: 30)

The author of the epistle to the Hebrews says of Him:

"Seeing then that we have a great high priest, that is passed into the heavens, Jesus the Son of God; let us hold fast our profession. For we have not an high priest which cannot be touched with the feeling of our infirmities; but was **in all points tempted** like as we are, **yet without sin**." (Hebrews 4:14-15)

The Apostle Peter testified in the house of Cornelius the centurion to those gentiles whom would believe:

> "The word which God sent unto the children of Israel, preaching peace by Jesus Christ: (he is Lord of all) That word, I say, ye know, which was published throughout all Judaea, and began from Galilee, after the baptism which John preached;
>
> How God anointed Jesus of Nazareth with the Holy Ghost and with power: who **went about doing good**, and healing all that were oppressed of the devil; for God was with him." (Acts 10: 36-38)

Others said of the Lord:

> "And when the devil was cast out, the dumb spake: and the multitudes marvelled, saying, It was never so seen in Israel." (Matthew 9: 33)
>
> "...And it came to pass, when Jesus had ended these sayings, the people were astonished at his doctrine: For he taught them as one having authority, and not as the scribes." (Matthew 7: 28-29)
>
> "And many of the people believed on him, and said, When Christ cometh; will he do more miracles than these which this man hath done?" (John 7:31)

Jesus demonstrated His anointing with power on many occasions as numerous miracles were performed as a testimony to all the nations of the earth, and for all generations. As Jesus approached the culmination of his earthly ministry with honor, he was aware that soon he would be betrayed, tortured, and executed.

The final words spoken to his disciples as they gathered together for Passover established a "new pact", remembered by believers today in the taking of Communion.

The Bible tells us:

> "And as they were eating, Jesus took bread, and blessed it, and brake it, and gave it to the disciples, and said, Take, eat; this is my body. And he took the cup, and gave thanks, and gave it to them, saying, Drink ye all of it; For **this is my blood of the new testament**, which is shed for many for the remission of sins." (Mathew: 26: 26-28)

We spoke previously of the covenant made with Moses as the mediator. **This pact** required the shedding of blood of an innocent animal, which was then sprinkled on the people. Moses told them, *"Behold, the blood of the covenant..."* (Exodus 24: 8)

We also recall that this covenant was shattered:

> "...the house of Israel and the house of Judah have **broken** my covenant which I made with their fathers."
>
> (Jeremiah 11:10)

God promised thru Jeremiah: "...saith the LORD, that I will make a **new covenant**..."   (Jeremiah 31: 31)

The Lord Jesus here states: **"the blood I shall now shed will be sufficient to seal the new covenant."**

There will be no animal sacrifice; but **God incarnate in Jesus Christ** will give his life. Jesus had to shed his blood and dying in this manner was the only death possible for him. The death of Jesus Christ would be as prophesied; as his blood flowed from his body.

As we read in the Book of Hebrews:

> "And almost all things are by the law purged with blood; and **without shedding of blood is no remission**."   (Hebrews 9: 22)

He could not nail his own hands on the cross, or pierce his own side so as the blood would flow and be poured out. Others had to crucify him in sacrifice and it was only reasonable that those God had given the commandment of Passover would be the ones calling for His death, in

34

fulfillment of prophesy. As the Messiah of Israel had spoken; "This is the **blood of the New Covenant**... *shed for the remission of sins*."

The judgment of a Holy God required that Jesus the Christ shed his blood. There is no longer any need for any sacrifice. The price has been paid for sin. The power of the blood of Jesus appeases our God and grants us His favor.

As the Jewish Apostle Paul wrote:

> "Purge out therefore the old leaven, that ye may be a new lump, as ye are unleavened. For even Christ our Passover **is sacrificed for us**: Therefore let us keep the feast, not with old leaven, neither with the leaven of malice and wickedness; but with the unleavened bread of sincerity and truth." (1 Corinthians 5: 7-8)

It bears repeating once again, there is **no longer any sacrifice required** as our Father allowed His only begotten Son to be slain by sinners, and thru faith in Him we are cleansed. Jesus is the Lamb of God without blemish who gives eternal life to those born of the Spirit thru faith in the redeeming power of that blood.

We are then **empowered** to **live a pleasing life** before God, which is our reasonable service.

The Bible says:

> "Furthermore then we beseech you, brethren, and exhort you by the Lord Jesus, that as ye have received of us **how ye ought to walk and to please God**, so ye would abound more and more. For ye know what commandments we gave you by the Lord Jesus.
>
> For this is the will of God, even your sanctification, that ye should abstain from fornication: That every one of you should know how to possess his vessel in sanctification and honour; Not in the lust of concupiscence, even as the Gentiles which know not God: That no man go beyond and defraud his brother in any matter: because that the Lord is the avenger of all such, as we also have forewarned you and testified. For God hath not called us unto uncleanness, but unto holiness." (1Thessalonians 4: 1-7)

At this juncture, let us recall that **two covenants** were made between God and His people. The first was **circumcision** and the second was the **shedding of blood** for sin.

We just spoke of the New Covenant in the blood of the Lamb of God. There is another covenant that now illuminates our understanding regarding circumcision. This will be our focus now.

36

THE COVENANT OF CIRCUMCISION IS REPLACED

A characteristic of the persona of Jesus Christ when on this earth was his adamant opposition to the religious leaders that were responsible for instructing the Jewish people in the law and righteousness. He frequently denounced them as **hypocrites** and exposed them as insincere and duplicitous. (*Example- Matthew 23: 1-36*)

There was one instance the exchange between the Lord and teachers of the law became intense:

"...They answered him, **We be Abraham's seed**, and were never in bondage to any man: how sayest thou, Ye shall be made free?

They answered and said unto him, Abraham is our father. Jesus saith unto them, **If ye were Abraham's children**, ye would do the works of Abraham....Ye do the deeds of your father. Then said they to him, We be not born of fornication; we have one Father, even God. Jesus said unto them**, If God were your Father**, ye would love me: for I proceeded forth and came from God; neither came I of myself, but he sent me.

...**Ye are of your father the devil**, and the lusts of your father ye will do. He was a murderer from the beginning, and abode not in the truth, because there is no truth in him. When he speaketh a lie, he speaketh of his own: for he is a liar, and the father of it."

(John 8: 33-44)

John the Baptist had admonished the leaders before this:

"Bring forth therefore fruits worthy of repentance, and begin not to say within yourselves, We have Abraham to our father: for I say unto you, That God is able of these stones to raise up children unto Abraham."

(Luke 3:8)

Afterwards, **Apostle Paul** wrote concerning Jewish believers who felt secure they were saved due to circumcision:

"...For circumcision verily profiteth, if thou keep the law: but if thou be a breaker of the law, thy circumcision is made uncircumcision" (Romans 2: 25)

We understand by this the act of being born a legitimate Jew does not guarantee the person is walking with God, and **circumcision is inextricably connected** to obedience to God's moral law.

We read clearly in Romans 2:25 that circumcision is beneficial if the condition of obedience to the law is met (**conditional**). Therefore, those circumcised on the eighth day must not transgress the law of God or they are considered uncircumcised.

It also can be said that Jews that are disobedient to God's law are no different under the law than gentiles that are uncircumcised.

As we further read in the same chapter 2 of Romans:

"Therefore if the uncircumcision keeps the righteousness of the law, shall not his uncircumcision be counted for circumcision? And shall not uncircumcision which is by nature, if it fulfil the law, judge thee, who by the letter and circumcision dost transgress the law? For **he is not a Jew**, which is one outwardly; **neither is** that **circumcision**, which is outward in the flesh: But he is a Jew, which **is one inwardly**; and circumcision **is that of the heart, in the spirit**, and not in the letter; whose praise is not of men, but of God" (Romans 2:26-29)

In summation, it can be said that circumcision cannot justify if the law is not kept. This is what Apostle Paul writes, inspired by God- the Holy Spirit:

"For in Christ Jesus neither circumcision availeth anything, nor uncircumcision, but a new creature." (Galatians 6:15)

The impact is significant here in that all who takes pride in being "circumcised on the eighth day" are confronted by this specific scripture and its ramifications. He tells them all that "if you keep the law, circumcision is of great value; but if you are a transgressor, you receive nothing."

They must decide whether to come to a realization of this truth or be offended by it.

We are reminded of the person who this truth was revealed to, and how he wrote of his own life:

"Though I might also have confidence in the flesh. If any other man thinketh that he hath whereof he might trust in the flesh, I more: Concerning zeal, persecuting the church; touching the righteousness which is in the law, blameless." (Philippians 3: 4; 6)

This revelation was given to Paul after the death of our Lord on the Cross of Calvary, and he instructs us that the covenant of circumcision was a mystery that had "Not been fully understood." We are given to understand that God seeks those that are circumcised of **heart**. The purity He seeks is **internal**, not external. Outward appearances can easily deceive and holiness is not measured by any superficial, external behavior. God once told the Prophet Samuel:

> "But the LORD said unto Samuel, Look not on his countenance, or on the height of his stature; because I have refused him: for the LORD seeth not as man seeth; for man looketh on the outward appearance, but the LORD looketh on the heart." (1 Samuel 16:7)

God scrutinizes the heart... "for he is not a Jew who is one outwardly, nor is circumcision that which is external and of the flesh." For some, Paul's writings at first glance may seem in contradiction to the pact made with Abraham that we read in Genesis 17: 10-14. What Paul has tells us explains the spiritual revelation of the covenant of circumcision and its deeper meaning.

This is what he reveals to us:

> "Not as though the word of God hath taken none effect. For they are not all Israel, which are of Israel: Neither, because they are the seed of Abraham, are they all children: but, In Isaac shall thy seed be called. That is, They which are the children of the flesh, these are not the children of God: but the **children of the promise** are counted for the seed.For this is the word of promise, At this time will I come, and Sara shall have a son." (Romans 9: 6-9)

Here Paul writes of how Abraham had **two sons**, one of the flesh and the other of the promise. Those born of the promise are the true heirs of the Patriarch (though others may make that claim of their own accord).

In the epistle to the Galatians we read this explanation:

> "Tell me, ye that desire to be under the law, do ye not hear the law? For it is written, that Abraham had two sons, the one by a bondmaid, the other by a freewoman. But he who was of the bondwoman was born after the flesh; but he of the freewoman was by promise. Which things are an allegory: for these are the two covenants; the one from the Mount Sinai, which gendereth to bondage, which is Agar." (Gal 4:21-24)

Paul wrote there of the **specifics** of the promise and its **limitations**. In Romans he sheds light on the gentiles (those not born Jews).

> "Now I say that Jesus Christ was a minister of the circumcision for the truth of God, to confirm the promises made unto the fathers: And that **the Gentiles might glorify God** for his mercy; as it is written, For this cause I will confess to thee among the Gentiles, and sing unto thy name." (Romans 15:8-9)

He continues writing:

42

"And again, Esaias saith, There shall be a root of Jesse, and he that shall rise to reign over the Gentiles; in him shall the Gentiles trust." (Romans 15:12)

Christ Jesus came as a servant of the circumcision... who revealed the truth of God and confirmed the promises made to the fathers. God in Christ fulfilled all that was written of Him for the salvation of the Jews and the tearing down of barriers between Jew and Gentile.

The Gentile can seek and find the God of Israel and praise His name! As **Christ was circumcised in the flesh**, <u>all Gentile believers are circumcised through Him</u> whether this was actually done on them as babes or not. Christ the "Righteous" is our justification and he gave his life.

We now live in him and thru faith can enjoy the promise of abundant life, blessings, and purpose.

The Bible says:

"And ye are complete in him, which is the head of all principality and power: In whom also ye are circumcised with the circumcision made without hands, in putting off the body of the sins of the flesh by the circumcision of Christ:" (Colossians 2:10-11)

Gentile believers now inherit the promises given to Abraham at the time the covenant of circumcision was first established. Jesus Christ is all we need for peace with God, and because of Him we are complete.

JESUS CHRIST, OUR RIGHTEOUSNESS

We have read where Apostle Paul explains that in the spiritual realm, for a Jew to truly be complete and fulfilled it *is required that he **keep all** the law.*

> "Therefore if the uncircumcision keep the righteousness of the law, shall not his uncircumcision be counted for circumcision? And shall not uncircumcision which is by nature, if it fulfil the law, judge thee, who by the letter and circumcision dost transgress the law? For he is not a Jew, which is one outwardly; neither is that circumcision, which is outward in the flesh:
>
> But he is a Jew, which is one inwardly; and circumcision is that of the heart, in the spirit, and not in the letter; whose praise is not of men, but of God."
>
> (Romans 2: 26-29)

Being conceived and born from the womb of a Jewish mother is not sufficient. There are Jews that practice the rituals, observe the feast days, and zealously seek to follow all written in the Law of Moses. These are **truly Jewish**; in the traditional sense.

There are others that are secular and follow little or no Jewish tradition. Paul writes that spiritually; they **cannot** really be considered Jewish. He also lets us know that those gentiles that had formerly lived a life apart from God in a disorderly fashion can draw near and know Him. Although they were not heirs of the promises and alienated from God, thru faith in Jesus Christ they are now circumcised! We are compelled to fully comprehend the great blessings afforded the gentiles in Christ. Apostle Paul writes in his letter to the Romans:

> "Brethren, my heart's desire and prayer to God for Israel is, that they might be saved. For I bear them record that they have a zeal of God, but not according to knowledge. For they being ignorant of God's righteousness, and going about to establish their own righteousness, have not submitted themselves unto the righteousness of God. For Christ is the end of the law for righteousness to every one that believeth."
>
> (Romans 10: 1-4)

45

Here we read how Israel seeks thru obedience to the law the condition of righteousness and consequently acceptance by God. They presently continue **to strive** to **keep all** the ordinances and precepts but are not able to. It is **not possible** to achieve. Nevertheless, a Holy God desires that they might comprehend the meaning and significance of the sacrifice of Messiah (Christ), and the righteousness of God would then be attributed to them in Christ. When we accept that the whole law was lived out and fulfilled in Jesus Christ; He is our righteousness.

We dwell in **Jesus Christ the Righteous**. He was perfect in all and our faith in him allows our heavenly Father to say, "... by being covered by him, you are also perfect thru him." It is written that all who confess and believe in him shall be saved.

> "For **there is no difference between the Jew and the Greek**: for the same Lord over all is rich unto all that call upon him. For whosoever shall call upon the name of the Lord shall be saved." (Romans 10 12-13)

We recognize that we can never obtain God's favor with our own efforts, strive as we may. We must seek, accept, and appropriate the righteousness of God given to us thru Christ as mediator and apprehend this benefit thru faith.

JEW OR GENTILE? HOW ARE WE DIFFERENT?

The Bible reveals that those in Messianic Judaism can keep the ordinances of the law as well as practice the rituals given by God to Abraham and Moses. A Messianic believer that is born from a Jewish womb, circumcised on the eighth day, practices the rituals, and celebrates the festivals is keeping the traditions of the fathers.

He can continue to keep them always as is Jewish custom, but has a choice when Jesus is accepted as Lord and Savior. He can choose to remain worshiping in the Jewish context as a believer in Jesus, and **not have to "convert" to Christianity**. The gentile believers are commonly known as the "church" of God in the world or the "body of Christ."

This is the Bible narrative of Apostle Paul's first journey back to Jerusalem after his encounter with the Lord on the road to Damascus.

> "And when we were come to Jerusalem, the brethren received us gladly. And the day following Paul went in with us unto James; and all the elders were present.

47

And when he had saluted them, he declared particularly what things God had wrought among the Gentiles by his ministry. And when they heard it, they glorified the Lord, and said unto him, Thou seest, brother, how many thousands of Jews there are which believe; **and they are all zealous of the law**:" (Acts 21:17-20)

We read here that any Jew that accepts Jesus as Messiah receives the grace of God and is justified thru faith in Christ. He or she is then saved and **can continue in the Jewish traditions** if they so please. That is a choice.

We recognize that knowledge of the law and keeping of feast days can justify no one before God; though it is understood there are significant lessons in all ordained by God. It is correct to continue to serve the Lord in Jewish context, and this choice does maintain alive the witness of faith in Messiah for the Jewish mindset and culture.

By the same token, a Jewish believer may not want to continue in their tradition and thus desire to worship with gentile believers in unity. **No one** in Christ **must continue to keep** days, seasons, or rituals. It may not even be feasible to find a Messianic Temple or group near them. As we have stated, Messianic Judaism is a choice for the Jew that accepts Christ, as well as worshipping with fellow believers that are non-Jewish. This is the choice only given to Jewish believers. There is a vast difference between a modern day judaizer and a Jewish believer who lives in grace.

A conversation with a born again believer might be along these lines:

- "Are you Christian?"
- "Yes."
- "Did you know that Christ was a Jew?"
- "Yes I did."
- "Then you must also become a Jew."
- "Why?"
- "The Jews are G-d's people and you are required to be Jewish to be a part of Israel and be saved"…

My friend, this is totally different than what we've said is the choice of the Messianic Jew. I wish to make everyone aware of what is happening and all should be on the alert.

Many false teachers have gone out under the guise of being Jewish and attempt to change right teaching and in effect confuse Christians. They charge that we must become followers of tradition and be Jews. This cancer is infecting congregations in Latin America and worldwide.

They confuse some of the more gullible brothers and use scare tactics that cause believers to doubt their own salvation. These are the contemporary judaizers. They approach us with subtlety and are determined to force us into the law of rituals and Jewish customs. THIS IS COMPLETELY WRONG. They ignore grace and would have us believe we must convert to a distorted Judaism to receive salvation.

The modern day judaizers attempt to dismiss the new covenant in Jesus Christ and the power of the precious blood shed for the remission of sin. They entice and persuade those drawn away that only by seeking to live out the 613 regulations, statutes, and precepts can a person become a Jew, and thus part of the covenant people of God.

All they teach is false. The Bible says:

"Stand fast therefore in the liberty wherewith Christ hath made us free, and be not entangled again with the yoke of bondage. Behold I Paul say unto you, that if ye be circumcised, Christ shall profit you nothing. For I testify again to every man that is circumcised, that he is a debtor to do the whole law. Christ is become of no effect unto you, whosoever of you are justified by the law; ye are fallen from grace." (Galatians 5: 1-4)

The truth is revealed to us in the Word of God so that no one might be deceived. He that preaches contrary to the light of revelation is in darkness and lies. We must reject this perversion of the gospel of truth. The Bible clearly lets us know that Jew and gentile both have access to the Father of light.

> "And came and preached peace to you which were afar off, and to them that were nigh. For through him **we both** have access by one Spirit unto the Father. Now therefore ye are no more strangers and foreigners, but fellow citizens with the saints and of the household of God;" (Ephesians 2: 17-19)

> "**Having** therefore, brethren, **boldness to enter into the holiest** by the blood of Jesus, By a new and living way, which he hath consecrated for us, through the veil, that is to say, his flesh; And having an high priest over the house of God; Let us draw near with a true heart in full assurance of faith, having our hearts sprinkled from an evil conscience, and our bodies washed with pure water." (Hebrews 10: 19-22)

We must be careful and not give in to the judaizers who are leading many to false teaching and supplanting the sound doctrine we have already accepted.

Nothing more should be added to what there is revealed in the Holy Bible. More time than not, they eventually end up confessing their denial of Christ as the God-man sent to redeem mankind. They have dismissed the Divine nature of the Person of the Holy Spirit and the veracity of the Biblical cannon accepted by scholars, and its divine inspiration.

To them there is no Trinity in the God-head. Their religiosity influences those that are easily impressed by external appearance. Theirs is an astuteness of the flesh and manipulation so common in the world system.

We have never witnessed true adherents to Judaism enter a Christian church to proselytize, and I believe we never will. Nevertheless, the judaizers enter our midst dressed as Jews and without hesitation begin to preach these strange doctrines. If as a believer you encounter one, I ask you to question them openly, "Were you born a Jew?" This is **the key** and signals their intentions.

A dialogue with one may go this way:

- "Sir, what congregation do you belong to?"
- "Where are they located?"
- "Were you born Jewish?"
- They may answer, "No, I converted"...

If we discern a false teaching it is our responsibility to expose it, as gently as possible. If it becomes necessary we can expose any false teacher by saying, "You are not a Jew, and you are an impostor."

Let us remember this counsel from the Bible:

> "Beware lest any man spoil you through philosophy and vain deceit, after the tradition of men, after the rudiments of the world, and not after Christ. For in him dwelleth all the fulness of the Godhead bodily. And **ye are complete in him**, which is the head of all principality and power" (Colossians 2: 8-10)

This is the good news: We are complete in Christ and no longer slaves to the law. We have all we'll ever need in Christ; everything. As a child of God our assurance is in Jesus. Christ overcame and we are free. Let us remain this way and protect the liberty we have. As we had written, Paul continues to teach the Colossians and says Christ fulfilled all the law and in him we are circumcised.

> "In whom also ye are circumcised with the circumcision made without hands, in putting off the body of the sins of the flesh by the circumcision of Christ: Buried with him in baptism, wherein also ye are risen with him through the faith of the operation of God, who hath raised him from the dead." (Colossians 2: 11-12)

We have sinned and deserve eternal separation from God but Christ took our sin upon himself at Calvary. Our sin was nailed on the Cross and He says: *I died for all mankind so that all may live.* He died for the forgiveness of the sins of all who would accept this truth. Paul continues:

> "And you, being dead in your sins and the uncircumcision of your flesh, **hath he quickened together** with him, having forgiven you all trespasses; **Blotting out the handwriting of ordinances** that was against us, which was contrary to us, and took it out of the way, nailing it to his cross; And having spoiled principalities and powers, he made a shew of them openly, triumphing over them in it." (Col 2: 13-15)

The Lord Jesus Christ was nailed to a cross and all that stood in the way that we draw near to God was removed. He kept all the law and our debt is forgiven and forgotten. All demonic influence was defeated and He has all authority and power over all things. During the Roman Empire crucifixion was the mode of execution for the worst criminals. A sign was placed on the top of the cross to specify the reason for this extreme punishment and all who witnessed were able to read the offense committed by the condemned. This gave testimony that Roman law had been violated.

54

We are no longer guilty and that sign has been removed. Jesus annulled the decree of guilt we deserved by taking the punishment upon himself on that cross.

We should meditate on this carefully. Those guilty of being fornicators, thieves, and murderers are proclaimed innocent. All who have not kept every part of the Holy law of God can ask for forgiveness and turn away from sin and shame. We are saved by grace and are no longer condemned. Our Lord claimed the death warrant of every repentant soul as his own... took it upon himself, and the nails that went thru him removed our sentence of death. If anyone seeks to condemn or kill... there is no indictment written against us. The words are gone away and the paper is completely blank, white, and clean... What happened? Another One has paid the debt we had. This is what the Bible says: "those in Christ are promised abundant life." In light of this, Apostle Paul exhorts to continue in the grace of God and not allow this to be taken from us. He writes:

> "**Let no man therefore judge you** in meat, or in drink, or in respect of an holyday, or of the new moon, or of the Sabbath days: Which are a shadow of things to come; but the body is of Christ. **Let no man beguile you of your reward**..." (Col 2: 16-18)

Jesus Christ removed all that opposed and offended God, giving us **the right to be exonerated** and no man can judge those in Him.

If we are asked why we don't celebrate feast days or otherwise follow Jewish tradition there is a simple answer. *"We are not compelled to keep Judaic customs and we now live in grace".*

I would add this:

> "For he is our peace, **who hath made both one**, and hath broken down the middle wall of partition between us; Having **abolished** in his flesh the enmity, even the law of commandments contained in ordinances; **for to make in himself** of twain one new man, so making peace; And that he might reconcile both unto God in one body by the cross, having slain the enmity thereby"
>
> (Ephesians 2: 14-16)

What does our God tell us here thru Paul?

We all know that religious and Orthodox Jews are convinced they are the only people chosen and set apart by God. They spend their whole life being taught the impossibility of an unclean gentile inheriting the promises of God. Jesus of Nazareth was born a Jew of the line of Judah.

He obeyed Jewish law and customs such as feast days to perfection, and was sinless. Before giving up his life and shedding his blood there was no fault in Him. **After his sacrifice** the wall of division was removed and both Jew and gentile are justified only thru faith. We can all receive grace and salvation and only a rejection of this grace offered can separate us from God and each other.

WE ARE ALL PART OF A NEW FAMILY

"...For through him **we both** have access by one Spirit unto the Father. Now therefore ye are no more strangers and foreigners, but fellowcitizens with the saints, and of the household of God" (Ephesians 2: 18-19)

All those that will believe belong to the fellowship of saints and are members of the family of God. We cannot find where it is imperative to become Jewish. As the family of God we are the **children of God** and members of the Body of Christ.

After the death and resurrection of the Lord Jesus there was reconciliation and we are one.

Those saved are now united thru faith and justified thru grace. In Christ we became the chosen people and children of the Almighty. All those who have ever been born are able to approach the throne of grace and be saved; whether born a Jew or a gentile. Let us seek wisdom to comprehend our privilege in Christ and then with confidence reject all the wiles of the enemy; specifically the false teaching of the judaizers. In demonstration of the anointing we are equipped and resolute, and will firmly respond, "I **am not interested**."

I would pause here and once again clarify that I'm in no way referring to true Messianic believers, born legitimate Jews. My warning is against those not born Jewish that would pervert the gospel of grace and repentance from dead works, and replace it with justification thru adherence to tradition and the shadow of righteousness revealed in the law of Moses. Some of them had accepted grace and were saved, but now for their own convenience choose to teach wrongly and wreak havoc in the church of God.

To reiterate, they enter our congregations <u>on the pretext of teaching Jewish culture</u> and attempt to persuade whoever may listen to join a synagogue or some such gathering; whatever they may call it.

We may label them, "Christian judaizers", or even "evangelical judaizers." We would not identify them as "Messianic Jews" due to the fact they reside in confusion and most are not Jewish.

We define a Messianic Jew as a person born of a Jewish mother. In their zeal to seek God and after hearing the gospel, they were illuminated and came to understand the promises and prophesy of Messiah ben David in the Old Testament was accomplished in Jesus Christ. They come to the knowledge of Him that was able to keep all the law and not falter. His grace is accepted and they publicly declare that Jesus, or his Hebrew name Yeshua, is Messiah and their Savior. They believe the testimony of the New Testament and can be called Messianic Jewish believers.

In the course of this study we have proposed that **many who confess to be** Messianic believers **are in error**. They are Protestants with an ambiguous understanding of what conversion to Judaism or Messianic Judaism is.

> *(As Christians we should be clear on this key point. Not all those that speak or sing in Hebrew or have grown beards are Messianic Jews... including some who preach.)*

Again I emphasize that a Jewish person might seek God and wait for the messiah, and one day the veil of their understanding is removed and they give testimony of having faith in Jesus as Messiah. This person is saved! The actions of the contemporary judaizers are offensive to any authentic person identifying with Messianic Judaism. They may be called out as a "sham" and blasphemous. Jewish believers may confront any impostor and inquire:

- "Are you Jewish?"
- "Yes"
- "What family or tribe? Was your mother Jewish?" "What is her parentage or lineage?"
- "Did you say you converted "x" years ago?" "How was that? Etc.

I'm sure they would quickly inform them they are not Jewish. They may consider them a proselytizer or sympathizer. If a proselytizer they may inquire if they entered "**through the door.**" They might also call them a "**righteous proselytizer.**" It is certain they would not count them as a Jew. There are two alternatives available for the person interested in converting to Judaism. They can choose to **keep some** ordinances and this is considered "**entering thru the door.**"

The other choice is complying with the ritual of circumcision and observance of all the law. They are a "**righteous convert**." The distinctions are important.

PETER AND PAUL: DIFFERENT MINISTRIES

We read that Peter was called as Apostle to the Jews and his ministry was mainly to them, in Jerusalem. They observed the law and practiced circumcision. Most of the first Apostles remained in Jerusalem, Judea, and Samaria. They were the first Messianic Jews.

We then read that Paul was a scholar of Jewish law but was set apart to preach the gospel to the gentiles and not his own nation. His ministry did not impact among the Jews. Paul elaborated in this respect:

> "But contrariwise, when they saw that **the gospel of the uncircumcision** was committed unto me, as the **gospel of the circumcision was unto Peter**; (For he that wrought effectually in Peter to the apostleship of the circumcision, the same was mighty in me toward the Gentiles:)

And when James, Cephas, and John, who seemed to
be pillars, perceived the grace that was given unto me,
they gave to me and Barnabas the right hands of
fellowship; that we should go unto the heathen, and
they unto the circumcision" (Galatians 2: 7-9)

The Apostle recognizes that the depth of revelation
bestowed to him was not shown to the writers of the Old
Testament. The mystery had been entrusted to him and
he communicated this:

"...How that **by revelation** he made known unto me
the mystery... the mystery of Christ) Which in other
ages was not made known unto the sons of men, as it
is now revealed unto his holy apostles and prophets by
the Spirit; That the Gentiles **should be fellow heirs**,
and of the same body, and partakers of his promise
in Christ by the gospel... (Ephesians 3: 3-9)

This is the mystery that fills us with great joy and teaches
us of the unity of all in Christ. Gentile believers are not
preferred over Messianic Jews and none is superior to the
other. We are all equal!

Apostle Peter expands on this in one of his letters:

"And account that the longsuffering of our Lord is
salvation; even as **our beloved brother Paul also**
according to the wisdom given unto him hath

written unto you; As also in all his epistles, speaking in them of these things; in which are some things hard to be understood, which **they that are unlearned and unstable wrest**, as they do also the other scriptures, unto their own destruction. Ye therefore, beloved, seeing ye know these things before, **beware lest ye also, being led away with the error of the wicked, fall from your own steadfastness**. But grow in grace, and in the knowledge of our Lord and Saviour Jesus Christ. To him be glory both now and for ever. Amen." (2 Peter 3: 15-18)

Let's examine what Paul encountered as he traveled and entered the homes of the gentiles in his ministry. He was in constant fellowship with them and breaking of bread. At one point the judaizers of his day forced him into a confrontation. Paul was a devout Jew but we see him moving freely among gentiles. What was his response when they tried to intimidate him? Many were accepting Christ by faith and some Jews arrived and attempted to impose their errant dogma.

The historical narrative is found in the 15th chapter of the Book of Acts: "And certain men which came down from Judaea taught the brethren, and said, Except ye be circumcised after the manner of Moses, ye cannot be saved." (Verse 1)

The conversation may have gone something like this today:

> "What did you say? We don't know about circumcision." (They had totally been unaware of any such ritual).
>
> Judaizer: Do you believe in Messiah?
>
> New Believer: Yes, glory to God.
>
> Judaizer: Do you also think you are saved?
>
> New Believer: Yes, amen.
>
> Judaizer: Have you been circumcised?
>
> New Believer: What is that?
>
> Judaizer: Don't you know what circumcision is? You must cut the foreskin... to be a part of the covenant made by God with Abraham. If you don't obey and perform this ritual you cannot inherit the promises and be considered as part of the body of Christ.
>
> New Believer: Paul never mentioned any of this.
>
> Judaizer: Well, now you know and it must be done!

Imagine the alarm and chaos this "news" brought them!

> "When therefore Paul and Barnabas **had no small dissension and disputation** with them, they determined that Paul and Barnabas, and certain other

of them, should go up to Jerusalem unto the apostles and elders about this question." (Verse 2)

"And when they were come to Jerusalem, they were received of the church, and of the apostles and elders, and they declared all things that God had done with them. But there rose up certain of the sect of the Pharisees which believed, saying, That it was needful to circumcise them, and to command them to keep the law of Moses." (Verse 4-5)

I will highlight some of what is recorded of the meeting of the First Council of the Church in Jerusalem. I recommend you continue to read the whole chapter. The brother of Our Lord, James, was one of the principle leaders and this is what he said:

"Wherefore my sentence is, that we trouble not them, which from among the Gentiles are turned to God: But that we write unto them, that they abstain from pollutions of idols, and from fornication, and from things strangled, and from blood." (Verses 19-20)

Peter then recounts his experience after speaking to Cornelius and his household. Paul speaks of his encounter with the Lord, and then James concludes: "It is not necessary for the gentile believers to keep our traditions. I would insist obedience to four requirements."

- They do not worship idols or contaminate themselves eating food offered in sacrifice to idols. This practice is done as an offering to devils. 1 Corinthians 10: 20

- They must no longer be in fornication and sexual relations are good when in the context of what God ordained. They cannot be frivolous about this and must realize promiscuity is sin. Sexual intercourse is the palpable demonstration of the union between a man and woman joined in holy matrimony.

- They cannot eat any animal that has been strangled

- They do not eat the blood of any animal.

> [Any animal slaughtered by strangulation retains blood after dying; and we cannot consume blood. There are ethnic dishes of blood we must avoid.
> Ex. Blood sausage]

Paul never gave permission to partake of these dishes when he wrote:

"Whatsoever is sold in the shambles, that eat, asking no question for conscience sake. For the earth is the Lord's, and the fulness thereof." (1 Cor 10: 25-26)

The Holy Spirit gave this commandment to Christians thru the Apostles:

> "For **it seemed good to the Holy Ghost**, and to us, to lay upon you no greater burden than these necessary things; That ye abstain from meats offered to idols, and from blood, and from things strangled, and from fornication: from which if ye keep yourselves, ye shall do well, Fare ye well" (Act 15: 28-29)

The Bible is clear; the Holy Spirit in conjunction with the apostolic ministry insisted these were **the only restrictions** on the gentile believers. They were not Jewish and saved by grace thru Christ the Lord. If anyone were to add to this, we can say to them:"No thanks, we do not accept what you teach."

What is really puzzling and strange is that the gentile brothers accepted the demands of the judaizers instead of obeying the word given by the Holy Spirit. Paul was so distraught that he wrote:

> "I marvel that ye are so soon removed from him that called you into the grace of Christ unto another gospel: Which is not another; but there be some that trouble you, and would pervert the gospel of Christ."
>
> (Galatians 1: 6-7)

The Galatians believed those that taught contrary to Paul and acknowledged their doctrine as correct. They so quickly strayed from the truth that he wrote:

> "I marvel and am in shock, how can this be? Further on he fiercely admonishes them: O foolish Galatians, who hath bewitched you, that ye should not obey the truth, before whose eyes Jesus Christ hath been evidently set forth, crucified among you? This only would I learn of you, Received ye the Spirit by the works of the law, or by the hearing of faith? Are ye so foolish? **having begun in the Spirit,** are ye now made perfect by the flesh?" (Galatians 3: 1-3)

It is crucial to that we understand the salvation of a person in Christ is what's at stake and in the balance! The Word of God says:

> "For as many as **are of** the works of the law **are under the curse**: for it is written, Cursed is every one that continueth not in all things which are written in the book of the law to do them." (Galatians 3:10)

We accept the teaching, that whoever is under the law is no longer justified by faith. If you want to live by the precepts and ordinances of the past given to the Hebrew people; **this is your decision.**

The Bible is clear on this. If you decide to accept the grace of God and rest in Him without the burden of the law and weight of its consequences, these verses are for your benefit and peace of mind.

> "**Christ hath redeemed us from the curse of the law**, being made a curse for us: for it is written, Cursed is every one that hangeth on a tree: That the blessing of Abraham might come on the Gentiles through Jesus Christ; that we might receive the promise of the Spirit through faith." (Gal 3: 13-14)

I accept the death of Christ and recognize he died for you and me; though we were not born Jewish. By faith we obtained the promises and the Holy Spirit dwells in our heart.

We are **not proponents of ignoring the moral law found in the Ten Commandments**. In addition to this eternal law; there was a <u>ceremonial law</u> along with priestly functions. This was given to the people of Israel and was a shadow of things to come until Messiah is revealed to all who have lived.

The Ten Commandments are the law of God written in our hearts. They are all fulfilled by this law:

"Jesus said unto him, **Thou shalt love the Lord thy God** with all thy heart, and with all thy soul, and with all thy mind. This is the first and great commandment. And the second *is* like unto it, **Thou shalt love thy neighbor as thyself.** On these two commandments hang all the law and the prophets" (Matthew 22: 37-40)

"Owe no man any thing, but to love one another: for **he that loveth** another **hath fulfilled the law.** For this, Thou shalt not commit adultery, Thou shalt not kill, Thou shalt not steal, Thou shalt not bear false witness, Thou shalt not covet; and if there be any other commandment, it is briefly comprehended in this saying, namely, Thou shalt love thy neighbour as thyself. Love worketh no ill to his neighbor: therefore **love** *is* **the fulfilling of the law**" (Romans   13: 8-10)

"For in Jesus Christ neither circumcision availeth anything, nor uncircumcision; but **faith which worketh by love.**" (Galatians 5: 6)

Let us proceed with caution and respond to the warning given in the Word of God: *"A little leaven leaveneth the whole lump."* (Gal. 5:9)

Let us learn truth from the Bible. There is no room for any deception when we read and understand the Word of God.

Circumcision is not required to be right with God and a legalistic dogma will not save us.

Let us not fall from grace.

On one occasion Paul spoke these words to Peter:

> "We who are Jews by nature, and not sinners of the Gentiles, Knowing that **a man is not justified by the works of the law**, but by the faith of Jesus Christ, even we have believed in Jesus Christ, that we might be justified by the faith of Christ, and not by the works of the law: for by the works of the law shall no flesh be justified." (Galatians 2: 15-16)

He clearly discerned the difference between a Jewish believer and a gentile abiding in Christ obedient to God. In Jewish tradition and education the fear of God taught and is prominent. Most gentile culture allows for the enjoyment of temporal pleasures that lead to excesses. The rationale is the importance of *"living life to the fullest."* God is not consulted in daily experience and is not revered.

The great challenge Paul confronted as Apostle to the gentiles was to introduce the invisible God of Israel to an idolatrous and superstitious people.

They would have to be taught and helped on the way towards gaining an understanding of God and honoring Him with the example of their new life in Christ.

The gentiles could not continue in their former manner of living after accepting Christ as Savior. They had to allow themselves to be instructed and were molded as the clay to the potter in surrendering to the perfect will of God.

As Jewish people are already taught the fear of God, on receiving the Messiah Jesus they are guided into a more perfect understanding and testify they are now complete Jews. This is not the case in gentile culture. They must begin to learn the fear of God.

As we read the epistles of Paul we recognize his ministry as a **teacher**, or rabbi, to the gentiles that were before in darkness but have been transplanted to the kingdom of light.

> "Who hath delivered us from the power of darkness, and hath translated us into the kingdom of his dear Son" (Colossians 1: 13)

The main thrust of Paul's ministry was to teach, teach, and teach; combined with intercessory prayer.

How should we respond as gentile believers?

✦ Learning to live right.

Paul teaches us:

> "That ye **put off** concerning the former conversation the **old man**, which is corrupt according to the deceitful lusts; And **be renewed in the spirit of your mind**; And that ye **put on the new man**, which after God is created in righteousness and true holiness."
>
> (Ephesians 4: 22-24)

> "And be not conformed to this world: but be ye transformed by the renewing of your mind, that ye may prove what is that good, and acceptable, and perfect, will of God." (Romans 12:2)

Paul receives the capacity to enlighten us and I thank God for using this man who was an expert in Jewish culture, Pharisee of the Pharisees, and once persecutor of the Church. He had been jealous for Judaism, but was called as the instrument of God to teach those that were not; but now are, the children of God.

Before we finish this brief study I present the words of Apostle Peter:

> "But **ye are** a chosen generation, a royal priesthood, an holy nation, a peculiar people; that ye should shew

forth the praises of him who hath called you out of darkness into his marvellous light: Which in time past were not a people, but **are now the people of God**: which had not obtained mercy, but **now have obtained** mercy." (1 Peter 2: 9-10)

We proclaim how wonderful our Lord Jesus Christ is. He called us out of the darkness and thru His power, we no longer submit to the "prince" of this fallen age. Because of Jesus Christ our thoughts are different. Our values and priorities have changed. Why is this? We have believed in Him and the promise of the Comforter has been accomplished in us. The Holy Spirit is our teacher in all righteousness.

We have become the rightful children of God and heirs of the promises given to Abraham. This is not thru natural birth or circumcision, but **as a result of faith in the Son of God**. This is what is written in the Bible; Hallelujah!

We ought to always remain grateful to God for grace, and being liberated from the requirements of Mosaic Law. We are hidden in Christ and able to please God without the weight of the Pharisaic demand to keep all 613 requirements of the law. Thank you Lord!

Therefore, our response is sure for those who *would willingly and knowingly deceive*; the Word of God. Of course, the pangs of compassion are felt in the love of God. The Bible gives us a mandate on dealing with those that stray from sound doctrine:

> "Brethren, if any of you do err from the truth, and one convert him; Let him know, that he which converteth the sinner from the error of his way shall save a soul from death, and shall hide a multitude of sins."
>
> (James 5: 19-20)

> "Brethren, if a man be overtaken in a fault, ye which are spiritual, restore such an one in the spirit of meekness; considering thyself, lest thou also be tempted." (Galatians 6: 1)

This prayer can be used as a model for anyone in that situation:

> "Lord, open their spiritual eyes..." Yes Father, they are doing harm but have the potential for good. Open their eyes as you did with Paul."

Paul went about determined to do much harm to the Church and zealously persecuted them, but one day his spiritual eyes were opened. He then became an instrument for good in edifying the body of Christ.

There may be those in error that sincerely believe they are doing something good and now know "the truth."

Unfortunately they have fallen from grace and are under the curse of legalism. May the mercies of God deliver them and God grant them understanding.

As we reflect on these things we can intercede for those born Jewish. May we skillfully minister the gospel truth without pressuring them to "convert" to Christianity.

Our hope is for their reconciliation and salvation thru Jesus the Messiah. If they continue in Messianic Judaism we pray for their joy; as the Anointed One they longed for has arrived.

Our desire is their integration into the body of Christ. The Church is one body and there is no wall of separation and let it be known, all men and women from every nation, tribe, or tongue can be saved.

Those in Christ Jesus are one!

HIS PRIESTHOOD AND OURS

Nearing the end of his earthly ministry the Lord Jesus spoke to his disciples and explained:

> "And whither I go ye know, and the way ye know. Thomas saith unto him, Lord, we know not whither thou goest; and how can we know the way? Jesus saith unto him, I am the way, the truth, and the life: **no man cometh unto the Father**, but by me." (Juan 14:4-6)

In this dialogue He shows them the Aaronic **priesthood is about to change.**

His disciples had been taught that Moses and the tribe of Levi were chosen as priests to intercede for the people before God. The law was given to Moses and was the "way" the people would draw near and communicate with God. They received guidance, grace, and forgiveness thru obedience. Instructions followed on the form of celebration in the Tabernacle of Meeting and Aaron was chosen, (*the older brother of Moses*) with his children and descendants for the office of priests. They would minister to the people.

Aaron would be called as High Priest and after his death one of his sons would continue. This line of succession was given.

God had told Moses:

> "And take thou unto thee Aaron thy brother, and his sons with him, from among the children of Israel, that he may minister unto me in the priest's office, even Aaron, Nadab and Abihu, Eleazar and Ithamar, Aaron's sons." (Exodus 28:1)

> "And the LORD said unto Moses, Speak unto **the priests the sons of Aaron**, and say unto them, there shall none be defiled for the dead among his people... They shall be holy unto their God, and not profane the name of their God: for the offerings of the LORD made by fire, and the bread of their God, they do offer: therefore they shall be holy... Thou shalt sanctify him therefore; for he offereth the bread of thy God: he shall be holy unto thee: for I the LORD, which sanctify you, am holy... And **he that is the high priest among his brethren, upon whose head the anointing oil was poured**, and that is consecrated to put on the garments, shall not uncover his head, nor rend his clothes... Neither shall he go out of the sanctuary, nor profane the sanctuary of his God; for the crown of the anointing oil of his God is upon him: I am the LORD." (Leviticus 21: 1-12)

78

Order was establishes and only those authorized by God participated, and ministered to Israel. There is an interesting detail regarding priestly access before God. Elohim (God) commanded there be restrictions; among them:

ONE: THE VEIL

God instructed Moses:

> "And thou shalt **make a vail** of blue, and purple, and scarlet, and fine twined linen of cunning work: with cherubims shall it be made: And thou shalt hang it upon four pillars of shittim wood overlaid with gold: their hooks shall be of gold, upon the four sockets of silver. And thou shalt hang up the vail under the taches, that thou mayest bring in thither within the vail the ark of the testimony: and the vail **shall divide** unto you between the holy place and the most holy"
>
> (Exodus 26: 31-33)

TWO: PLACE OF MINISTRY

> "And thou shalt make **an altar** to burn incense upon: of shittim wood shalt thou make it ...And thou shalt put it before the vail that is by the ark of the testimony, before the mercy seat that is over the testimony, where I will meet with thee." (Exodus 30: 1-6)

THREE: EXACT TIME OF YEAR FOR SACRIFICES

"And Aaron shall make an atonement upon the horns of it **once in a year** with the blood of the sin offering of atonements: once in the year shall he make atonement upon it throughout your generations: it is most holy unto the LORD." (Exodus 30:10)

"And the LORD said unto Moses, Speak unto Aaron thy brother, that he come not at all times into the holy place within the vail before the mercy seat, which is upon the ark; that he die not: for I will appear in the cloud upon the mercy seat." (Leviticus 16:2)

"And this shall be an everlasting statute unto you, to make an atonement for the children of Israel for all their sins once a year. And he did as the LORD commanded Moses." (Leviticus 16:34)

THERE ARE NO RESTRICTIONS IN CHRIST!

Remember what Jesus spoke to Thomas the Apostle:

"Jesus saith unto him, I am the way, the truth, and the life: **no man cometh unto the Father**, but by me." (John 14:6)

The prophetic word had to be fulfilled and Matthew writes concerning these events:

80

"Jesus, when he had cried again with a loud voice, yielded up the ghost. And, behold, **the veil of the temple was rent in twain** from the top to the bottom; and the earth did quake, and the rocks rent" (Matthew 27: 50-51)

The author of Hebrews later writes:

"Which hope we have as an anchor of the soul, both sure and steadfast, and **which entereth into that within the veil;** Whither **the forerunner is for us entered, even Jesus**, made an high priest for ever after the order of Melchisedec." (Hebrews 6:19-20)

"For Christ is not entered into the holy places made with hands, which are the figures of the true; but **into heaven** itself, now to appear in the presence of God for us: Nor yet that he should offer himself often, as the high priest entereth into the holy place every year with blood of others; For then must he often have suffered since the foundation of the world: but **now once in the end of the world** hath he appeared to put away sin by the sacrifice of himself."

(Hebrews 9:24-26)

"For by one offering he hath perfected for ever them that are sanctified. Whereof the Holy Ghost also is a witness to us:

For after that he had said before, This is the covenant that I will make with them after those days, saith the Lord,

> I will put my laws into their hearts, and in their minds will I write them; And their sins and iniquities will I remember no more.

Now where remission of these is, there is no more offering for sin"   (Hebrews 10: 14-18)

This is the good news of the Gospel. There is a High Priest in Heaven who loves us so much that He gave his life in demonstration of this love.

It is written in the Bible:

> "But God **commendeth** his love toward us, in that, while we were yet sinners, **Christ died for us.** Much more then, being now justified by his blood, we shall be saved from wrath through him."   (Romans 5:8-9)

Jesus sits on the right hand of the Father as triumphant; and able to intercede for all who trust in Him (Heb 1:3)

> "But this man, because he continueth ever, hath an unchangeable priesthood. Wherefore he is able also to save them to the uttermost that come unto God by him, seeing **he ever liveth to make intercession for them**."   (Hebrews 7:24-25)

As result, we are fully confident of that written in the Word of God:

> "Having therefore, brethren, boldness to enter into the holiest by the blood of Jesus, **By a new and living way**, which he hath consecrated for us, **through the veil, that is to say, his flesh**; And having an high priest over the house of God; Let us draw near with a true heart in full assurance of faith, having our hearts sprinkled from an evil conscience, and our bodies washed with pure water" (Hebrews 10:19-22)

Jesus offered His own body on the tree and has torn asunder the veil of the temple. There is **only one Way** to the Father: **JESUS CHRIST – SON OF MAN** (1Timothy 2:5)

In addition to this **all believers in Him** are called as holy priests; not being Levites (Exodus 28:1; Leviticus 21:1-12); but now as part of the priestly family of our Lord, who calls us "His brothers"

> "For both he that sanctifieth and they who are sanctified are all of one: for which cause **he is not ashamed to call them brethren**" (Hebrews 2:11)

> "And from Jesus Christ, who is the faithful witness, and the first begotten of the dead, and the prince of the kings of the earth. Unto him that loved us, and washed us from our sins in his own blood, And hath made us

kings and priests unto God and his Father; to him be glory and dominion for ever and ever. Amen."

(Revelations 1:5-6)

Glory to God for Jesus and Hs indescribable grace!

I urge you to exercise the authority placed in you as a priest of God. Jesus Christ, our High Priest hears your supplications in intercession. The Holy Spirit *(Ruach Ha Kodesh)* guides us in all truth here on earth.

BLESSINGS:

> *"The LORD bless thee, and keep thee: The LORD make his face shine upon thee, and be gracious unto thee: The LORD lift up his countenance upon thee, and give thee peace."* (Numbers 6:24-26)

> *"The grace of the Lord Jesus Christ, and the love of God, and the communion of the Holy Ghost, be with you all. **Amen**"*

(2 Cor 13:14)

Other books Author has published

(Available in English and Spanish)

If at any time you have asked yourself:

- What has happened to Christianity?

- Where is the brightness that illuminated the mind of man for many centuries past?

- How is it that the power of the teaching of sound doctrine has diminished in these end times?

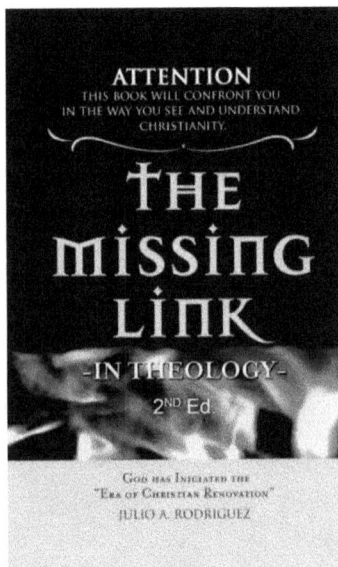

ATTENTION
THIS BOOK WILL CONFRONT YOU
IN THE WAY YOU SEE AND UNDERSTAND
CHRISTIANITY.

THE MISSING LINK
-IN THEOLOGY-
2ND Ed.

GOD HAS INITIATED THE
"ERA OF CHRISTIAN RENOVATION"
JULIO A. RODRIGUEZ

- What events occurred and caused much denominational rivalry and religious sects?

- Is there a possibility of salvation and life after death?

You will discover
Non-traditional answers
to these questions
in the pages of this book

The Paradigm, or Tale?

# of Evolution

A Christian-Scientific Research

Julio A. Rodríguez

An atheist for more than fourteen years and an ardent defender of the theory of evolution; the author is a graduate of the prestigious "Pontificia Universidad Catolica Madre y Maestra" in Santiago, Dominican Republic.

He graduated as a chemical engineer and continued to diligently investigate the theory of Evolution. Now thirty years later, with the insight of a scientist and countless experiences, he presents the logical conclusions set forth in this revealing book on Evolution.

The author assures us he can demonstrate:

"Educational institutions and Universities **indoctrinate** students with the purpose of removing faith in God, teaching an atheistic pseudo-science religion.", and: "If anyone were to accept that AN ATOM suddenly formed the entire universe, this person has **shown more faith** than those who confess their faith in God.

A must read for students and interested parents.

In what do you put your faith?

---

[i] All biblical references are from King James Version

[ii] Each emphasis given to any verse, either in **bold**, *italic* or <u>underlined</u> is added by the author.

www.ingramcontent.com/pod-product-compliance
Lightning Source LLC
Chambersburg PA
CBHW070549030426
42337CB00016B/2418